# My Life, My Choice, My Voice

## Emily Elizabeth Moore

**To order additional copies of this book, contact:**
Xlibris Corporation
1-888-795-4274
www.Xlibris.com
Orders@Xlibris.com
110969

*(1)*

I saw this in my dreams
I just don't know what it means?
My life
My Choice
My Voice

*(2)*

Do you know where
Cats are from
Heaven above
No Egypt
So how the hell
Do they know so much
About fish?
They must have been
Laying around on the beach of the Nile.

(3)

Have you ever had
To dissemble this
And then bend mad
What was had?
Life
You tell me?
Have you ever escorted dead bodies
Out the door?
I have
I guess I will
As was before.

(4)

I got sick of these worms
I got sick of these germs
I will not cross contaminate anymore
I am just sick of these worms.

*(5)*

The choice you feel
Do you feel
Does It make you real
I am not stupid
Not scared
I just want to know
What is real?

*(6)*

What's an impulse?
What's a whim?
Is it a sin?
Or
How close?

*(7)*

Sit around
And wait
Is that my fate?
Or
My faith?

*(8)*

Let me writing
Let my life
Be my life.

(9)

Something inspire you chef
Tried
Without reason
Was it fear?
Or hope
A better life
Was it waiting outside
Or
Lying in wait?

*(10)*

I want to do
What I love
The gift I was sent from above
Screw the best
Of this bullshit
You can laugh in my face
But
I will take your place.

*(11)*

I don't know it
So
I can't own it
Your life
Your life
Paid for?
In your tears.

*(12)*

Faith does not
Lie in wait
Fortunately or unfortunately
It is bigger
Than we are.

*(13)*

The wind was so
Strong that day
That I knew nothing
Would go unchanged.

*(14)*

The end of pain
Everything I thought
Everything I fought
Its either the Demons
Or the fruit flies.

*(15)*

Everything smells
Life etalon and pride
When you are by my side

*(16)*

Sometimes life
Cannot fit between lines

*(17)*

I may have been an easy score
Not anymore
I wanted a life
I wanted a wife
But I am not an easy score
You have nothing to teach
Except lies and cheats
I don't need it anymore
And I loved you
Really loved you
I don't think I do anymore
I hope I do anymore
I hope you make it
To the end of what?

*(18)*

I am not that sharp
I am not that pretty anymore
But there is something above me
You will not be able to ignore
I just found this is my sock drawer.

(19)

Waking up at 5 am
For what?
For what?

*(20)*

The outside is hard and prickly
The inside soft and sticky
Like the people you love
Like what is up above like God
Find the core
The pit
Maybe you won't wonder anymore
Maybe you won't wonder anymore
Maybe won't wonder anymore?

*(21)*

Out of the snakes mouth came
A bare ace of truth
Maybe you didn't listen
Because
It came out of the snakes' mouth
And they are snakes
Maybe because they don't have hands
Or feet
So stop and think
I have learned more from snakes
Than from you.

*(22)*

If I am going to
Make a mistake
And I am
Let me make it on
The side of love
Not the side of
Hate and fear.

*(23)*

Chicken baby
You make me crazy
But I will stand by
Your side
Take you to your land
If that is what you decide
Will I understand?
I love your hips
I love your lips
But that is not what
Makes me crazy
Chicken baby
I love your heart
The feel of your kiss
I love you chicken baby.

*(24)*

A scar on my heart
On my soul
When you go
All you did was tell lies
That not even you understood
I wanted you to be my wife
Not a knife in my back
So just know
When you go
You left a knife in my heart
And a scar on my soul.

*(25)*

I can love you
Or
I can leave you
It's your choice
Your voice
So tell me who you are
I already know
Who I am.

(26)

I remember the place
The smell
The look on your face
So why assign blame
To me?
To you?

*(27)*

I hate that the things I write
Come from spite
I am not that person
Not anymore
Just not anymore
Guess I am
With this pen in my hand.

*(28)*

It does not matter where I sleep
I pray the Lord my soul
To keep
Integrity what you do when
No one is watching.

*(29)*

When life knocks out
The key component you
Get to hear the background.

(30)

I know what it is
Like to have a fist
In your face
And a hand below your waist
Well I will tell you asshole
Your name is on my list.

*(31)*

I knew it too young
I knew it too old
So it scared my heart
And stole my soul.

*(32)*

Does it rhyme?
Off the tip of my tunic
Does it make you
Come undone
The venom I swap is for me
Not you
But it mess you come undone
Because it is true
Off the tip of my tunic.

*(33)*

The wake of destruction
And the wake of craze.

(34)

Understand your soul
What is there to be hold?
If there is nothing then let it go
There is must left to be told
God let it just be unrest.

*(35)*

In your eyes
Your lies
I am scares
And lies
But I have always been here
Have I hidden my face
When I have felt despite
Maybe but
I have always been here
Despite my fear
I have tried despite your lies
I love you now
And
I will love you again
Despite your lies.

*(36)*

Writing or cleaning
I don't know
One day neither will
Matter anymore
I will still have my sores
Will you have yours?

*(37)*

These dreams are my feelings
I pray that they are not a waist
I didn't pray to hate you
I love you more
Is that a waist?
I live for tomorrow
Knowing it will bring sorrow
Will it ?
Answer me.

*(38)*

For once in my life
Let me do something right
Write.

*(39)*

Sometimes you have
No idea what some else
Feels inside /inside
Their head, heart, soul
Hell their feet, shoulders
And sometimes you do
But I can't tell
Their stories, only mine
Or can I ?

(40)

There are no mistakes
Except the ones we make
Integrity dignity
Second only to kindness.

*(41)*

Seven virgins or
Seven whores
What's the count
In heaven anymore
I know my strife
But not your life
Seven virgins or
Seven whores
I don't care anymore
You're not my wife
In this life
Maybe just my whores
Was I right?
I hope not.

*(42)*

I sold my grief
I sold my fears
But they are still here.

(43)

Jesus Christ I don't know
God
Let me love, let me live
Let me believe that
What I did
Was right
Was it ?

*(44)*

It's just not worth it anymore
Settle down
Can you hear the peace?
Of some relief
Or just the grief
In your bones
In your soul
I don't know anymore
But settle down
It's not worth it anymore.

*(45)*

Do I want the serenity?
Or do I want the hit
I really don't know.

(46)

I have been hurt immeasurably
It hurts me immeasurably
That you think
I love you for what you do
Not that I don't
But I love you for
Who you are
Who you are
And no that is not
My slave, my caretaker
Nor my child
I love you just because
And you hurt just because
But I love you anyway !